Developing sex and relationships education in schools

Guidance and training activities for school governors

Gill Frances and Paula Power

Sex Education Forum

The Sex Education Forum is the national authority on sex and relationships education. The Forum was established in 1987 and is based at the National Children's Bureau. It is an umbrella body bringing together over 50 national organisations involved in sex and relationships education. Member organisations work together to share good practice, and to articulate a common voice in support of sex and relationships education for all children and young people.

National Children's Bureau

The National Children's Bureau promotes the interests and well-being of all children and young people across every aspect of their lives. NCB advocates the participation of children and young people in all matters affecting them. NCB challenges disadvantage in childhood.

NCB achieves its mission by:

- ensuring the views of children and young people are listened to and taken into account at all times;
- playing an active role in policy development and advocacy;
- undertaking high quality research and work from an evidence based perspective;
- promoting multidisciplinary, cross-agency partnerships;
- identifying, developing and promoting good practice;
- disseminating information to professionals, policy makers, parents and children and young people.

NCB has adopted and works within the United Nations Convention on the Rights of the Child.

Published by the National Children's Bureau, Registered Charity number 258825.
8 Wakley Street, London EC1V 7QE. Tel: 020 7843 6000.
Website: www.ncb.org.uk

© National Children's Bureau, 2003
Published 2003

ISBN 1 904787 02 9

British Library Cataloguing in Publication Data
A catalogue record for this book is available from the British Library.

Contents

Foreword

I am delighted that *Developing sex and relationships education in schools: Guidance and training activities pack for school governors* has been developed. Through my years of being in education and a school governor, I know how seriously governors take their responsibilities and how useful this pack will be.

The factsheet answers governors' questions; the book provides authoritative guidance on the governors' role and responsibilities and offers a range of activities for working with governors. The video is excellent; it really demonstrates the enthusiasm and the commitment of schools and governors to SRE.

Current Government legislation and guidance, research findings and the evident support from school communities offer an excellent context for ensuring children and young people's entitlement to SRE. The links between positive health and well-being and effective learning are emerging from research as well as practice. There is no better time for developing effective SRE policy and practice than now.

Melody Dougan
National Association of Governors and Managers
September 2003

Acknowledgements

Thank you to all the people who shared their time and expertise so generously in participating in the filming and making of the video and in drafting and piloting the pack. We want to give our special thanks to all the children and young people who shared their views with us, especially those from:

Baden Powell Primary School, London Borough of Hackney; Shepherd Special School, Nottingham; Wickersley Secondary School, Rotherham.

We want to say thank you to the Advisory Group:

Simon Blake, National Children's Bureau; Martyn Carr, National Children's Bureau; Roz Caught, National Healthy School Standard; Hilary Dixon, Independent Consultant; Carol Glover, Headteacher, James Barrie Primary School; Kay Lord, National Health Education Group; Baroness Massey, Chair of Governors, James Barrie Primary School; Carol Marriott, APAUSE; Sarah Thistle, Redbridge LEA; and Marilyn Toft, National Healthy School Standard.

Also, thank you to all those who piloted the pack:

Graham Hoffman, Tessa Parkinson, John Cornish, Jude Clements, Lynne Howie, Lynne Devine, Katie Hall, Stella Muttock, Andre Sinclair, Alison Cockerill, Clare Laker, Christine Woods, Majid Ali, Greg Cooper, Ant Flanagan, Vivence Quant, Sarah Hazlehurst.

We want to give special thanks to Melody Dougan, of the National Association of Governors and Managers, who advised on the project and with gentle insistence made sure that the finished product would be really helpful to governors; and to Michael Merwitzer and Siân Williams and their team from KOSH for their excellent film and for being fun to work with.

Thank you to Mark Dunn for project administration and a special thank you to Tracey Anderson for her 'eye for detail' in the administration of the pack's development.

And finally, we are extremely grateful to the Department for Education and Skills, the Teenage Pregnancy Unit and the Department of Health for funding this project and for their support throughout; especially Karen Turner, Lucy Fogarty and Sue Pentland.

About the authors

Gill Frances is Director of Children's Development at NCB and Deputy Chair of the Independent Advisory Group on Teenage Pregnancy. She has many years experience of promoting children's entitlement to sex and relationships education and Personal, Social and Health Education and Citizenship across all aspects of their lives at home, school, and in care, secure and community settings. She has written and contributed to a wide range of publications as well as delivered PSHE and Citizenship to children, young people, their parents and school governors.

Paula Power is an independent training consultant in all aspects of Personal Social and Health Education and advises and trains teachers, parents, governors and youth workers. She has many years experience as an inner city secondary school teacher, advisory teacher and Healthy School Coordinator. She has developed several local authority sex and relationships guidance documents and has written articles and resources on all aspects of PSHE and Citizenship. She is a school governor.

1 Introduction

A good governor is someone who believes children and young people have an entitlement to effective SRE and is prepared to prod their governing body into taking on that responsibility and to encourage the head teacher and Senior Management Team to keep it on the agenda.
governor adviser

They (governors) are key players, supporting staff and helping parents – they are 100 per cent behind us.
head teacher of a special school

About the pack

Developing sex and relationships education in schools: Guidance and training activities pack for school governers is for people who work with and support governors. It includes a video, book and a factsheet.

- *SRE: Support for school governors* is a 17-minute video, which shows how schools are developing SRE in partnership with governors, school staff, parents, pupils, health professionals and the wider school community. It can be used in governors' meetings and in school planning meetings, twilight training sessions, multi-disciplinary courses, seminars and conferences as a trigger for discussion.

- *Developing sex and relationships education in schools: Guidance and training activities for school governors* is a book which provides:
  - information about governors' role, best practice, policy development, partnership and participation;
  - a range of training and support activities that can be used in a mix and match way at governors meetings, in workshops, seminars and conferences;
- *Sex and relationships education: support for school governors* factsheet (which can also be downloaded from www.ncb.org.uk/sef, see also Appendix 1) contains answers to commonly asked questions from school governors and can be used as:
  - a stand-alone leaflet for governors which can be disseminated at meetings,
  - support for training, seminars and conferences,
  - stimulus in a training sessions;

- *Talk to Your Children About Sex and Relationships* is a leaflet for parents (which can be downloaded from www.ncb.org.uk/sef, see also Appendix 2) that provides answers to commonly asked questions and can be used as:
  - a stand-alone leaflet that can be sent home when planning SRE,
  - support for events and meetings with parents,
  - support for parents who want to withdraw their child from SRE.

This book concludes with the learning outcomes for SRE at all Key Stages suggested by Ofsted, and lists of useful organisations and resources.

About the project

The Governors and SRE project was developed by the Sex Education Forum in partnership with National Association of Schools Governors and Managers (NAGM). We worked with schools across England interviewing governors, head teachers and senior managers, teachers, parents, school nurses and, most importantly, children and young people. All the material was developed from what is actually happening in schools today. The draft pack was tested by governors and people who train and support them. The filming was directed and produced by KOSH, a performing arts production company that specialises in creating live theatre performances and community education video programmes (see Useful organisations, page 91). KOSH has a great deal of experience of working in schools and is deeply committed to children and young people's participation in the development of effective policy development and good practice.

It was very exciting and reassuring to see so much good practice and governor confidence in developing SRE policy in partnership with parents, pupils, staff and the school's wider community. Governors told us that although the work was sometimes challenging it was deeply rewarding once they had got over initial fears. Children, young people and their parents joined in, enthusiastically grasping the opportunity to give their views and offer positive and helpful suggestions.

Healthy School

It is clear that the development of Healthy School status is helpful in ensuring good quality SRE because it offers a context and structure for careful planning, effective policy development and partnership working. Healthy schools are also working hard to target those who are hard to reach and are making real progress in ensuring that the needs of some of our most vulnerable children are met, boys and girls, including young parents, those with physical and learning disabilities, those from minority ethnic communities and those who are lesbian and gay.

Need and context

Current research tells us that children and young people want SRE in schools; and parents want schools to provide SRE, to build on what they are trying to provide at home. Very few parents withdraw their children from SRE in school. We now have excellent and clear SRE Guidance from the Department for Education and Skills (DfES, formally DfEE) and a national Teenage Pregnancy Strategy, which is working towards reducing teenage parenthood and improving support for young parents. Ofsted has carried out a survey on school SRE and produced a report 'Sex and Relationships' (Ofsted 2002). It clarifies what should be included in the SRE policy, how it is best taught and makes a range of recommendations for policy development and practice. It also includes suggested learning outcomes for SRE at all key stages (See Appendix 3). It is hoped that all secondary schools will have a PSHE/SRE certificated teacher by 2005 and that all schools will become healthy schools. The context for developing SRE in schools is better than it has ever been and the need is greater if we want to ensure that this generation of children and young people leave school equipped with the skills and knowledge to maintain sexual health and well-being.

2 Working together to promote effective SRE policy and practice

Governors' role in SRE

Governors are concerned about fulfilling their role and the SRE and school governors project was able to identify key tasks and responsibilities.

Their statutory responsibilities include:

- overall responsibility for SRE policy development;
- ensuring that the policy is made available for parents and that it includes clear procedures for parental withdrawal;
- having regard to the SRE Guidance.

Best practice responsibilities include to:

- initiate and support the review of SRE policy on a regular basis; once every two or three years is advised. SRE is included as an agenda item at governors meetings on an occasional basis;
- identify a lead governor(s) to work more closely with the PSHE and Citizenship Coordinator and team in developing SRE policy and practice;
- ensure that SRE, as part of PSHE and Citizenship, is in the school development plan to secure adequate resourcing of SRE, and its coordination across the whole curriculum;
- support the staff, ensure that they are adequately trained to deliver SRE and that the SRE policy underpins effective practice. Teachers will also need strong support if there is a complaint regarding SRE;

They are learning about relationships ... they are learning to take responsibility.
governor secondary school

- work with parents, attend meetings with parents and listen to their views;
- support pupil participation in SRE policy and practice. Guidance from DfES on pupil participation and involvement for schools, governing bodies and local education authorities is forthcoming;
- support best practice in SRE by understanding the content of SRE, how it is best-delivered and encouraging schools to use Ofsted's recommendations for SRE including the SRE learning outcomes.

The four cornerstones of effective SRE

SRE is developed in the context of PSHE and Citizenship as recommended by DfES Guidance on SRE (0116/2000). It needs to be planned as part of a whole school ethos, which supports learning and teaching and emotional and social development. The four cornerstones of effective SRE are Participation, Partnerships, Policy and Practice. This section describes the various elements of the four cornerstones, and highlights the governors' role and responsibilities.

Ensuring participation

Because they're teaching about relationships, growing up, assertiveness, it has a knock-on effect in other subjects. Taking responsibility for their own lives and own learning.
secondary school governor

It's really amazing how children know what they want and how effective they can be in developing the programme.
primary school governor

Many children and young people are already engaged in the policy and practice development of SRE. There is a range of ways that pupils can be involved. They can:

- become a member of a Healthy School or SRE policy development task group;
- identify needs through carrying out surveys and interviews and collating them as part of the baseline data that informs policy and practice development and feedback to governors, teachers and parents;
- become involved in the school council to advocate for better SRE;
- become peer educators involved in delivering and supporting aspects of SRE;
- invite health professionals as visitors to the SRE lesson, briefing them and evaluating the session;
- visit the health services for young people in the wider community for the purpose of assessing their value and feeding back information to the school and the service itself;
- meet with governors to discuss SRE.

Governors have an increasing responsibility regarding participation. In some schools, governors invite pupils to their meeting and ask them to give a presentation and then join a discussion on either SRE or how participation using a range of activities supports SRE. In other schools, a lead governor on SRE consults with the school council or SRE peer education group.

Some people say our children are too disabled, I say it's their entitlement to learn about sex and relationships.
head teacher special school

Our Charter for good sex and relationships education

Every child has the right to sex education in all areas (gay, lesbian, straight, bisexual).
Every child has the right to express his or her opinion.
Every child has the right to specific information, advice, counselling and support.

To achieve this …

- we want society to be more open about sex in general
- parents should be able to talk to their children without feeling embarrassed
- there should be a special sex education team
- teachers who feel comfortable to give sex education should be given support, courses and workshops
- outside visitors should be allowed to come into schools

continued…

We would expect to learn about ...

- real-life dilemmas
- sexuality and relationship issues:
  - peer pressure
  - problems
  - friendships
  - being gay or lesbian
  - contraception
  - STIs
  - HIV
- pros and cons about sex
  - when is the right time to have sex?
  - where to go and get advice (for example Brook)
- we would like free booklets to take away.

We would like sex education to be fun ...
This would be through:

- role plays and games
- videos
- opportunities to explore dilemmas
- practising communication
- discussions that are open and multi-ethnic
- a comments and suggestions box allowing children and young people who would otherwise feel embarrassed to ask questions, and gives us a chance to say what we want to know
- using mechanical baby dolls.

We would like outside visitors to come and talk to us ...

- teenage mothers
- a lesbian or gay man
- people with different life experiences to express
- people from clinics

Children and young people have the right to be involved and participate in their school and the wider community. The UN Convention for the Rights of the Child states in Article 12 that 'children should be given opportunities to express their views on decisions that affect their lives'. The Education Act 2002 recognises this right. DfES will be publishing participation guidance for LEAs, schools and their governing bodies in the very near future.

Children and young people are already being consulted on all child-related national Government policy. The new Children, Young People and Families Directorate at DfES reflects this change of culture. Many schools are beginning to benefit from involving children and young people in the processes of running a school.

The Sex Education Forum has benefited from ensuring that children and young people participate in their policy and project work. A participation video *Sex, myths and education: Young people talking about sex and relationships education*, in which young people say what they want, is available from www.ncb-books.org.uk

A Charter for SRE was written by young people attending a National Children's Bureau Talkshop event on 26 February 2000. The Charter for SRE is reproduced on pages 8 and 9 and can be downloaded from ww.ncb.org.uk/resources/sexed_ypcharter.pdf

Working in partnership

Effective partnerships are proving essential for effective SRE policy and curriculum development. Groups and individuals who work in partnership with schools include:

- children and young people;
- parents/carers;
- school nurses;
- people from the wider community including voluntary sector workers and religious leaders;
- Primary Care Trusts, Local Education Authority, Voluntary Organisations;
- local Healthy Schools Partnership Coordinators;
- local business (for example to sponsor activities or to provide work experience opportunities);
- local statutory and non-statutory agencies (for example for provision of specialist resources, team teaching support);
- local coordinators such as Quality Protects Coordinators and Teenage Pregnancy Coordinators;
- national organisations who provide support materials, advice, support and information;
- youth workers, Connexions personal advisors, and mentors.

An SRE working group can be formed to develop effective policy and curriculum development in SRE. The lead governor can join such an SRE working group.

Developing partnerships with health and voluntary agencies

SRE should ensure that children and young people are informed about and assisted in accessing individual advice and support as and when they need it. In some cases this support may be available within the school through school nurses or other professionals. In others, this may not be available and, even where it is, children and young people may want to seek advice, care or treatment from specialist agencies outside the school. Through forging closer links with local services, schools can support children and young people and access expertise and accurate information about their needs, which can then be used to develop SRE. DfES guidance states 'that all young people need access and precise information about confidential contraceptive information, advice and services'. School staff can provide information through SRE and provide leaflets and contact information of health and advisory services, organisations and helplines on bulletin boards, in leaflets and other media. Involving local service providers in SRE as external visitors can help to promote awareness, knowledge and confidence about accessing services as part of planned SRE.

School staff and the governing body have a responsibility to promote the welfare of all the pupils and to keep them safe from harm. All visitors must work within the SRE and child protection policies. Visits to schools and planned visits to the services must be carefully negotiated and monitored by staff.

School nurses and other health professionals, of course, work within their own ethical guidelines when working individually with children and young people but they are expected to work within SRE policy when working in the classroom delivering SRE.

There are specific and age appropriate leaflets and booklets for younger children on growing up. Further information is available in *Secondary schools and sexual health services: Forging the links* (Thistle 2003).

School governing bodies that have invited health professionals to join the governing body have found it invaluable.

> *I work for the Primary Care Trust, it's really useful in my role as a governor.*
> secondary school governor

Governors also invite health professionals, often the school nurse, to talk with them about local sexual health needs and priorities. Many secondary schools have developed very effective partnerships with their Primary Care Trust and have developed a young people's advisory service in school or nearby in the wider community.

Working with parents

> *It's important that parents feel they also have a role in teaching the subject.*
> primary school teacher

> *We do have good relationships with the teachers, we are able to come in to talk one to one with a teacher. The head teacher is always on hand and because of this open door – that's where you get your confidence from.*
> primary school parent

Although parents want to talk to their children about sex and relationships, they often find it difficult and embarrassing and want schools to help them by providing good SRE. Surveys show 94 per cent of parents/carers support school-based SRE (NFER and HEA 1994). Only 0.04 per cent of parents choose to withdraw their children from SRE (Ofsted 2002).

Governors are required to make the SRE policy available to parents for inspection and to ensure that it describes the procedures for requesting that their child is withdrawn. Parents do not have the right to withdraw their child from the SRE element of the National Science Curriculum.

Reproduction is often taught within science. Parents do have the right to withdraw their child from elements of SRE provided within PSHE and Citizenship, which usually includes work on emotional and social skills development and values clarification. Ofsted has reported that children are very rarely withdrawn from SRE by their parents or carers.

In the unlikely event that parents do want to withdraw their child, teachers will need strong support from their governing body. The PSHE and Citizenship Coordinator and/or a senior manager should invite the parent(s) to talk through their concerns and to look at the materials and aims of the SRE provided. It is our experience that concerns are often based on a misunderstanding; a comment, picture or sentence taken out of context. Parents are usually reassured once the PSHE and Citizenship Coordinator and the parents have talked through the issue and the context, aims and values have been explored. However, if a parent does want to withdraw his or her child from SRE alternative arrangements will need to be made for the pupil during the time that the lessons are in progress. Young people can of course still access information on health services in the school or from public sources such as libraries, posters, leaflets and helplines. It may also be helpful to offer parents a leaflet.

Talk to your children about sex and relationships: support for parents (see Appendix 2) was developed in consultation with around 90 parents across the country. Commonly asked questions were identified and responded to in consultation with them. It is offered here in this pack for two reasons, one so that you know what questions may be asked and can be prepared with some answers and also as a leaflet for parents. It can be adapted to ensure that it meets a school's individual needs and priorities. It can be downloaded in a leaflet format from www.ncb.org.uk/sef

There are still some prevailing worries about working in partnership with parents as well as some assumptions that parents aren't interested. The occasional headline in a newspaper where a group of parents object to school education can wrongly confirm these fears. Unfortunately, all the success stories of schools and parents working together don't hit the headlines. It is our experience that many schools, governors and parents are working together confidently to ensure children's and young people's entitlement to SRE.

The SRE Guidance (DfEE 0116/2000) expects governors and schools to involve parents in the SRE policy.

> *If you have worked in a genuine partnership with parents, you've consulted them about the policy, made resources open to them, then they are very re-assured and actually relieved.*
> governor adviser

It is, of course, easier to work with parents around SRE if you have already established a partnership culture in school. Useful activities with parents include parent/teacher groups, parent governor groups, parents' evenings or community-based meetings.

The following are key features of successful partnership work with parents.

- Making meetings feel safe is important for teachers as well as parents. Ensure that there are clear aims, a planned structure and clear boundaries to enable discussion about SRE.
- Be open – be prepared to acknowledge if you're not sure about something, acknowledge it and work with parents to work it out.
- Remember that children come from different types of families and invite foster carers, grandparents and guardians.

- Try different times to ensure fathers as well as mothers can come and working and non-working parents can come.
- Ensure inclusion, an invitation to everybody in the school community may not feel inviting, it is alright to ask people individually if they want to join in and help.
- Accept that consensus is not necessary and disagreement is not a failure.
- Be clear about the school's values, the law and guidance affecting SRE.
- Be clear about the entitlement of children and young people to SRE, the health and education benefits for SRE and the school's aims and values for pupils' emotional and social development.
- Be sure to have some correct statistics about sexual health and teenage pregnancy – newspapers often mislead with incorrect information and 'shock horror' stories. Correct information is available from your Healthy School or Teenage Pregnancy Coordinators.
- Learn about different faith perspectives (*Faith, Values and Sex and Relationships Education*, NCB 2002).
- Avoid stereotyping. Statements such as 'parents won't come', 'teachers won't listen' aren't true and will get in the way of effective partnership work.
- Celebrate joint achievements.

In some areas parents have been trained as peer educators. Mothers and fathers talk to other parents about how to talk about sex and relationships to their children at home. They also work with schools, governors and teachers and contribute to the planning and delivery of SRE. The Parents Together from Sheffield and the Speakeasy project from fpa train and support parents. In Shepherd School for children with severe learning difficulties, the governors provide SRE training for parents.

Parentline Plus (see Useful Organisations, page 91) offers a telephone helpline for parents to get advice on how to talk about sex and relationships.

The following are some examples of activities for working with parents:

- Include SRE as part of a parents' evening focused on the more general subject of PSHE and Citizenship that addresses a range of personal and social issues such as growing up, coping with adolescence, alcohol and drugs.
- Include SRE as part of a session on 'working with girls' or 'working with boys'.
- Use a Healthy School celebration event to initiate a discussion on SRE.
- Work with pupils to present their ideas at a parents' meeting, which could be based on a school council activity of surveying pupils' SRE needs.
- Ask a group of peer educators to talk with parents and governors at a meeting.
- Include a short article on SRE in the school newsletter.
- Invite someone from outside the school to talk about a matter of concern to parents; perhaps from your local health promotion unit or Primary Care Trust; or someone from another school with successful experience.
- Organise class parents' groups, which move up the school with their children.
- Invite parents or grandparents into the classroom, to join in discussions, for example about being a parent or about their experiences of growing up in a previous time or another country.
- Run a 'health for families' open day or week, when school programmes, resources and examples of work are displayed as well as information or speakers from the local Primary Care Trust or organisations offering support on health and well-being.
- Set homework which requires pupils to talk and work together with their parents. Pupils in one primary school designed and used their own questionnaire with their parents.

- Use the school's parent network to spread the word. Running an interesting meeting will attract more parents to the next one.
- Put together a parents' pack to be available to all parents, but also to inform those who can't, or don't wish to come to a meeting.

It is essential that strong partnerships with parents are forged so that SRE can be developed confidently. It is not good practice or fair for children, young people and their families if schools avoid SRE because they are afraid of conflict. In all the schools we worked with we found that once teachers, governors and parents had got over their fears and often misconceived perceptions of each other they are able to work confidently and well together.

Developing policy

The status quo is not acceptable. To have such a high teenage pregnancy rate is not acceptable. To do nothing is not acceptable.
head teacher secondary school

As a governor it is your duty to make sure you are providing good SRE . . . think of young people not as 13-year-olds but as 23- or 33-years-olds, because as they get older life will be different for them.
head teacher special school

Governors have an overall statutory responsibility for SRE policy. They are not expected to write it but they are expected to initiate and ensure that the policy is reviewed on a regular basis at least once every two to three years. They should also ensure that SRE is part of PSHE and Citizenship and is included in the School Development Plan to secure adequate resourcing of SRE and its effective coordination across the curriculum. Although some schools are working towards a whole school policy for PSHE, as recommended in the SRE Guidance, some schools are finding it easier to develop separate policies for different aspects of PSHE which they keep in one folder. This may help them to develop an integrated PSHE policy next time.

The SRE policy addresses and includes:
- information about the school and the process for policy development;
- the aims of SRE;
- what aspects will be covered including reference to statutory requirements, good practice guidance and how it relates to school, local and national priorities;
- how it will be organised and delivered;
- how it will meet the needs of all pupils including those who are marginalised and vulnerable and need specific support;
- who is responsible for coordinating and delivering SRE as part of PSHE and Citizenship;
- the values framework for SRE within the school;
- how pupil learning will be monitored and assessed;
- how it links to other policies including confidentiality, child protection and bullying;
- how professional development needs will be identified and met;
- how the policy will be monitored and reviewed and when.

I am here today to talk to you about the differences between boys and girls.
community project worker in a primary school

Delivering best practice

You learn things about people you are going to meet, how to respect them, how to get on with them.
secondary school pupil

You could think there is something wrong if your friend has pubic hairs and you don't; but you are taught there is nothing wrong and everybody's different.
primary school pupil

Governors need to be confident they understand what is involved.
governor secondary school

Governors need to understand the content of SRE and how it is best delivered before they can develop effective SRE policy. Governors can also support effective curriculum development by encouraging schools to use the suggested SRE learning outcomes from Ofsted.

People who are trained will teach it more successfully than those who are not.
PSHE and Citizenship Coordinator secondary school

The Ofsted report also found that specialist teachers best deliver SRE. This means that teachers need training and governors can support this training by securing resources for it. DfES and the National Healthy School standard have developed a national

SRE is best delivered from the context of effective policy development. The following issues are considered during curriculum development.

- Is the curriculum for SRE relevant to children's development?
- Does the curriculum enable pupils to develop emotional and social skills and a positive attitude to health and well-being as well as acquiring information on sex, relationships and sexual health?
- Are the objectives for each lesson clear and specific?
- Is the curriculum challenging for pupils?
- Are a range of teaching methods used that match the aims and objectives of the curriculum and allow pupils to achieve at their own level?
- Does the curriculum build on prior learning? How is learning reinforced?
- How will pupil learning be monitored, assessed and progress recorded and reported?
- Will outside visitors be involved, if so how will you ensure the quality of the input?
- Are resources inclusive of all pupils?
- Will the classroom need rearranging to ensure a safe learning environment?
- How does it relate to other curriculum priorities such as ICT and literacy?
- Do appropriately trained staff deliver SRE?
- Are there opportunities for emotional and social development across the whole curriculum and how is it coordinated?
- What pastoral support is available and how will pupils know they can get help about sexual health and relationships?
- How are links and effective access made to confidential health services in the wider community?

SRE/PSHE certification for teachers and school nurses. For more information contact NHSS (tel: 020 7661 3072 or www.wiredforhealth.gov.uk).

Reviewing and developing SRE policy and practice: audit and review

The schools we worked with found it helpful if the lead governor on SRE joined a working group which leads on the development and review of SRE. Other members of the working group might include pupils, school nurse, health promotion staff, PSHE advisory teacher or Healthy Schools Coordinator, and representatives from community and faith groups, parents and carers, and Connexions advisors.

There are six main stages in the audit and review process of developing SRE policy and practice. The questions below can help in working through each stage.

Step 1: Identify how the development of SRE fits with other priorities

- Has SRE been discussed by the governing body? Has this review got the explicit support of the governing body? Is it on their current agenda?
- How does it relate to LEA Education Development Plans?
- How does it relate to local health priorities, for example teenage pregnancy, sexual health and emotional well-being?
- How does it relate to school priorities? How does it fit within the school development plan?
- How does it fit within healthy schools work?
- How will it support marginalised and vulnerable children and young people, for example those who are looked after?

Step 2: Review existing policy and practice

- How do the whole school ethos and values support a safe learning environment for SRE?
- What is the schools' existing policy on SRE? How does it meet national requirements and non-statutory guidance of PSHE and SRE? How does it take account of the differing needs of children and young people, for example the needs of boys and girls and those with a faith?
- How does it fit within the context of personal and social development opportunities offered within the school? How when, where and by whom is it delivered?
- What is the content of SRE? Does it have clear learning outcomes which address sex, sexuality, relationships, sexual health including faith and secular perspectives, social skills development and values clarification? How is the children and young people's learning and progress monitored and assessed?
- How are multi-agency partnerships established and how do these different partners contribute and add value to SRE?
- Is there a lead governor on SRE and how are governors involved in the review?

Step 3: Identify what the children, young people, parents, carers, the wider community and staff need and want from SRE

For all partners:

- What do these different partners need and want from SRE?
- What do they think of the existing programme? How do they think existing provision could be improved?

For pupils:

- Do they have opportunities to be involved in needs assessment, policy and curriculum development and delivery?

For staff involved in SRE:

- What aspects of SRE do staff feel confident in their knowledge of and skills in?
- How many staff members are trained to deliver SRE and what did the training consist of?
- What aspects are staff less confident with and what are their professional development needs? How will these needs be met?

For governors:

- Have governors been offered training and support? How can they be supported to feel confident and equipped to take overall responsibilities for SRE?
- Are governors involved in the process of review?
- Do governors understand to content, methodology and values framework of best practice in SRE?

Step 4: Identify local issues and trends

- What local issues need to be addressed within the programme, for example alcohol use and sexual risk-taking, teenage pregnancy, racism and homophobia?
- Do you have locally available data to inform you? For example school health profiling, teenage pregnancy data and sexual health data from the PCT, school improvement data from the LEA, and information from Connexions.

Step 5: Consultation and drafting policy

- Who will take responsibility for involving partners in the development of the SRE policy including the values framework?
  - How will children and young people feed into this process?
  - How will parents and carers feed into the process?
  - How will staff within the school, including teachers, learning support mentors, school nurses and the Senior Management Team, feed into the process?
  - How will people from the wider school community feed into the process?
- How will consultation take place on the draft values framework and policy?
- How will governors be consulted and agree the policy?
- How will governors ensure that the procedures for parental withdrawal are included?

Step 6: Implementing and monitoring the policy

- How will the policy be disseminated to children and young people, parents, carers, the community and all staff?
- What are the professional development needs of staff? (Do staff understand the role of SRE in reducing teenage pregnancy and improving sexual health?) How will professional development needs be met?
- Who will monitor the impact of the policy?
- When will it be reviewed?
- How will they ensure that SRE policy is available to parents?
- How will the evaluation of the policy be fed back to the governors?

3 Training and support

Working with governors

It is important to identify an initial way of interesting governors in SRE provision. Many schools will ask the PSHE and Citizenship Coordinator or school nurse to start the process of review and development of the SRE policy by having a 30-minute slot at a governors meeting. Using the video from this pack, *SRE: Support for school governors*, and leading a brief discussion can help to build confidence and interest and set the agenda for future work. The factsheet *SRE: Support for School Governors* will also be useful. Some school governing bodies have asked a group of pupils to do a small presentation and join them in a discussion of how SRE should be provided in school. Generally one or two governors are selected as lead SRE governors who become more closely involved in policy and curriculum development.

Governor-specific training can be provided locally either for an individual school or for a cluster of schools. The Sex Education Forum can provide a list of consultants who can provide training for governors (see Useful organisations). Training which is multidisciplinary and cross-phase is becoming increasingly popular. Spiral curriculum issues can be explored and understanding the different roles of teacher, school nurse and governor can be invaluable in future development of SRE policy and practice. In addition understanding the different needs of children and young people is very important. Governors need to know and understand what is being done at the different stages to ensure progression and effective policy and practice. And of course it is important for everybody to understand how colleagues working with children and young people with special needs are ensuring entitlement to SRE.

A range of training activities is provided in this section. They can be used flexibly, and be adapted and used in a mix-and-match way to meet local needs. All the activities have been tested with governors, teachers, PSHE and Citizenship Coordinators, Healthy School Coordinators and PSHE and Citizenship advisory teachers and consultants. All workshops should start with a warm up, finish with closure activity and be evaluated.

Running a workshop

Running a workshop with teachers, parents and governors needs careful planning. People give up their time and will want to achieve something that they can use to support SRE. These workshops are very enjoyable and rewarding. Some key points to remember in your planning are summarised here.

Preparation

- Find out the size, culture and language needs of the group, the shape of the room and seating arrangements and time available.
- Negotiate and agree aims and arrange who will receive feedback and the evaluation.
- Be clear about the governors' roles and responsibilities regarding SRE.

Planning

Having clear aims will help you to plan relevant activities and also reassure participants if they are a little nervous about the topic. They will also want some information on how you are going to run the workshop. Lengthy introductions can add to this nervousness so keep the introductory activities short, focussed on the workshop and not too intense.

Plan your activities so that people can:

- warm up and feel comfortable about being there once they know what they are there for, who else is there, what is going to happen and how;
- focus on the topic by offering an agenda building activity;
- engage with the issues by offering them an activity in which they can learn new information and skills;
- work out and plan how they can use the new information and skills by offering them an action planning activity;
- evaluate and assess the activity and reflect on their own learning and tell you what they have learnt.

Workshop programmes

Governors meeting
Time: 30 minutes
Activity C – Using the video *SRE: Supporting school governors*

Training for an individual governing body
Time: 2¹/₂ hours
Activity A – Working agreement
Activity B – Warm up
Activity C – Using the video *SRE: Supporting school governors*
Activity D – Setting the agenda
Activity H – Action planning

Training for a group of governors from different schools
Time: 3 hours
Activity A – Working agreement
Activity B – Warm up
Activity C – Using the video *SRE: Supporting school governors*
Activity D – Setting the agenda
Activity F – Clarifying the law and guidance affecting SRE
Activity H – Action planning

Training for a multidisciplinary group
Time: 4 hours
Activity A – Working agreement
Activity B – Warm up
Activity C – The video *SRE: Supporting school governors*
Activity D – Setting the agenda
Activity E – What should be taught and when
Activity F – Clarifying the law and guidance affecting SRE
Activity H – Action planning

Working with parents
Time: 1^1/$_2$ hours
Using Activity C – The video *SRE: Supporting school governors*
Activity G – Working with parents

The activities

Activity A: Working agreement

Making an agreement about how people will work together helps a group to feel safe to talk about the different aspects of SRE and to work towards a shared sense of values and commitment to SRE policy development.

Objective: to establish a climate which enables people to work together confidently.

Materials: Flipchart paper, felt-tip pens

Time: 15 minutes

Method

1. Ask the group to talk about what they need from each other to be able to talk about SRE.

2. Write up contributions on a flipchart to ensure clarity, shared understanding and agreement.

3. Ensure that the agreement is visible to all participants throughout the workshop.

Working agreement
We will:
Respect each other and each other's different opinions
Listen to each other
Not use jargon

Activity B: Warm up

It is important that people feel relaxed because there may be some initial fears. Getting to know people and knowing that everybody is there for similar reason often helps.

Objective: to get to know other people and feel relaxed and energised to start work.

Time: 15 minutes

Method

Ask people to move around and to meet as many people as possible talking to each person for a few minutes exchanging the following information:

My name is …
I am interested in this workshop because …
I am looking forward to …

Activity C: Using the video *SRE: Support for school governors*

The video is short and only lasts 17 minutes. It can be used in a range of settings. It is important that the video is not used as the only mechanism for supporting governors. It will interest people and probably raise more questions than answers. It is essential that there is time for discussion to further develop and plan the review and policy development process. It is good practice wherever possible to use video material as a trigger to further discussion and development of skills and knowledge in a structured and planned way. The video can be used in meetings of the governing body and in training events, seminars and small working group meetings.

It is usually possible to arrange a slot in a governing body meeting where the school PSHE and Citizenship Coordinator, Healthy Schools Coordinator or school nurse talks about SRE as an initial step to reviewing and developing SRE policy.

Objectives:

- to raise awareness of SRE and the governors' role in SRE policy development;
- to agree next steps for review and development of SRE policy.

Materials: video, TV and VHS machine, flipchart, Post-it notes, pens

Time: 30 minutes minimum

This activity can be extended to allow for more exploration of the issues that arise from the video.

Method option 1

1. Explain that they are going to watch the video *SRE: Support for school governors* and explain that it was made in different schools across England. It demonstrates how governors can fulfil their responsibilities to school SRE by working in partnership with teachers, parents and carers, and pupils. While watching the video ask the group to write down any comments or questions about the video on Post-it notes while they are watching the video.

2. At the end of the video – if you have time – ask people to get into pairs to discuss their observations and try to answer each other's questions.

3. In the group, ask people who still have questions to be answered to put their Post-it notes on a flip chart for all to see.

4. Use all the questions and comments to inform a whole group discussion about how to work with parents, pupils and teachers in the development of SRE policy and practice and how to make effective links with health services in school and in the wider community.

5. In the group ask what are the next steps: When and how will they take forward SRE? How can they support teachers? Can they identify a governor(s) who will lead on SRE by working with the PSHE and Citizenship Coordinator and link effectively with the governing body? How will they make effective links with the health services in school and in the wider community?

Method option 2

1. Explain that they are going to watch the video *SRE: Support for school governors* and explain that it was made in different

schools across England. It demonstrates how governors can fulfil their responsibilities to school SRE by working in partnership with teachers, parents and carers, and pupils. While watching the video ask the group to consider the following questions. What is SRE? What did the parents say about SRE? Why did teachers value the governors' support?

2. Respond to a few questions and if you only have 30 minutes ensure that you move fairly swiftly on to the next question.

3. In the group, ask what are the next steps: When and how will they take forward SRE? How can they support teachers? Can they identify a governor(s) who will lead on SRE by working with the PSHE and Citizenship Coordinator and link effectively with the governing body? How will they make effective links with the health services in school and in the wider community?

Activity D: Setting the agenda

Children and young people receive information about sex, sexual health, sexuality and relationships from a number of different sources from the moment they are born. Some of this information is correct and relevant for their age, stage of development and family culture. Other information can be incorrect, misleading and in some cases frightening. Current best practice ensures that children and young people have opportunities at home and in school to work out what is true, acquire correct information and develop their emotional and social skills so that they can feel confident when resisting pressures from others and in making decisions that affect their sexual and emotional health and relationships. It is important that governors understand why SRE is important and how SRE is taught so that they are able to develop effective policy.

Objective: to understand why SRE is important and to begin to clarify the content of SRE.

Materials:

Flipchart, felt tip pens

A selection of newspapers, both broadsheet and tabloid, and magazines targeting boys and young men as well as girls and young women.

Time: 45 minutes

Method

1. Ask people to get into pairs to recall how they learnt about sex, sexuality, sexual health and relationships. It may be difficult for some people and they will need support.

2. Ask them to discuss:
   - What did you learn about sex and relationships in the formal part of your education in primary or secondary school?
   - Was it what you needed at the time?
   - Who talked to you about sex and relationships when you were young?
   - Where else did you get information about sex and relationships?
   - Did you have any misconceptions or fears about sex when you were young? If so, what were they?
   - Did you get what you needed and on reflection how would you have liked your SRE to be?

3. Distribute some of the newspapers and magazines to each pair and ask them to look through them and talk about the current issues there are for children and young people? Do they think it is the same for children and young people today as it was for them? How is it different and similar for children and young people today? Where do children and

young people get their SRE from and how does it compare to what they received when they were young?

4. Ask each pair to join another pair and, in groups of four, to discuss the following questions and record their answers on flipchart paper.

   - What are the main issues for children and young people today?
   - How should the school respond, what do they want SRE in their school to offer the pupils?
   - What are the benefits for schools in developing effective partnerships with the local health services?
   - What do teachers need to be able to deliver good SRE?

5. In the group, ask people to identify the main points of SRE in their school.

Activity E: What should be taught and when

It is important that governors understand what needs to be included in SRE if it is to be relevant for children and young people.

Objective: to clarify what should be taught during each key stage.

Time: 45 minutes to one hour

Materials:

Topic Cards – a set for each small group, (see Appendix 4)
Suggested SRE learning outcomes from Ofsted, one copy for each small group (see Appendix 3)
Bluetac, Flipchart paper with the headings as follows:

Infants/Key Stage 1

Juniors/Key Stage 2

Secondary/Key Stage 3

Secondary/Key Stage 4

Key Stage 5

Method

1. Explain the activity and organise people into small groups working on one key stage and give them a pack of topic cards and a piece of flipchart paper with the headings listed above.

2. Ask individuals in each group to take turns to place a topic card in the key stage in which they think it should be taught within SRE.

3. When all the cards have been placed on the flipchart ask people if they want to positively challenge where a statement has been placed.

4. In the group, discuss how people experienced this activity.

5. Give each group a copy of the Ofsted handout (Appendix 3) and ask them to compare their list to the recommended SRE learning outcomes for each key stage.

6. Ask each group to feed back their findings to the plenary and describe where they have consensus and where there is disagreement.

7. Conclude with an agreement on how people will move forward to ensure that the SRE policy is helpful to the needs of children and young people and fits in with the Ofsted recommendations.

Activity F: Clarifying the law and guidance affecting SRE

Although SRE Guidance and legislation is summarised in the fact sheet in Appendix 1 people do find it helpful to work through this quiz. They can ask questions, consider the effect on school policy and practice and develop their confidence in knowing what is expected of them as governors.

Objective: to understand and to develop confidence in developing policy which is mindful of government legislation and guidance.

Materials:
SRE law and guidance quiz answer sheets (one per person, see Appendix 5), and pens

Time: 45 minutes to one hour

Method

1. Explain the purpose of the activity and ask people to attempt to answer the quiz on their own.

2. When everyone has finished answering the questions ask them to compare answers in pairs.

3. Go over the answers with the whole group, allowing time for discussion and debate. Encourage people to discuss their answers and clarify any uncertainties.

4. Finish by distributing the answer sheet (Appendix 5).

Alternatively, participants could be asked to fill in the question sheet at the beginning of a training session and re-visit it at the end to consider what they have learnt.

Quiz: Clarifying the law and guidance affecting SRE

Are the following statements true or false?	True	False	Don't Know
1. School governors have an overall responsibility for determining policy on both the content and organisation of SRE within the school.			
2. Governors are expected to work in partnership with the head teacher, pupils, staff, parents and health professionals and others from the wider community.			
3. Homosexuality is included throughout SRE.			
4. Contraception and abortion are included in SRE.			
5. SRE should link with the sexual health services in the school and in the wider community.			
6. Schools catering for students with special educational needs are expected to provide SRE.			
7. Parents have the statutory right to withdraw their children from SRE.			
8. All children have a statutory right to SRE.			
9. HIV/AIDS and other sexually transmitted infections are included in SRE.			
10. Schools can develop a confidentiality policy.			

Activity G: Working with parents

This activity has been included for those people who are facilitating a meeting with parents. In some schools governors have led meetings with parents and in other schools a joint meeting with governors and parents has been led by the PSHE and Citizenship Coordinator or school nurse. This is a very enjoyable way of learning about SRE and also developing effective partnerships.

Objective: to involve parents in deciding what their children need to learn about sex and relationships and to support future partnership working.

Material: Flipchart paper, pens and tape recorders (optional)

Time: one hour

Method

1. Ask people to work in pairs to talk about what they learnt about sex and relationships when they were the age their children are now, and whether they felt confident about sex and relationships when they were young adults.

2. Ask them to join another pair to talk about how their experience compares with what their children know now.

3. In the group, share some of the key local sexual health concerns and take questions. It is often helpful to ask a group of pupils or the school nurse to do a short presentation.

4. Back in the the small groups of four, ask them to work out what they want the school to provide and record it on flipchart paper or talk into a tape recorder. Those drafting the SRE policy can use this information.

5. In the group ask people to:
   - read each others' flipcharts or ask for a volunteer for feedback – be mindful of possible writing difficulties of those parents whose first language isn't English;
   - compare their ideas with the school's existing programme;
   - discuss any concerns parents may have about SRE;
   - confirm what they want their children to learn at school.

6. Ask for volunteers to support SRE policy development by: joining a working party; doing a survey of parents needs; being available for consultation on specific issues such as cultural or religious needs, the needs of boys and girls or sons and daughters with special education needs.

Activity H: Action planning

It is essential that all training includes action planning otherwise learning, however enjoyable, may not be used in future policy development. At the end of a course, people may feel enthusiastic but unclear about how to turn the learning into specific goals and actions. Action planning with clear indicators of support enables participants to see support as a necessity to effective action.

Objective: to develop an action plan which supports involvement and commitment to effective SRE policy development.

Materials:
- *SRE: Support for School Governors* factsheet (Appendix 1)
- Action planning sheet

Time: 30 minutes

Method

1. Ask people to refer to the section 'Where to start?' and the model PSHE and Citizenship policy framework in the factsheet *SRE: Supporting school governors* (Appendix 1) and to consider alone for a few minutes what they have gained from the course and ask them to identify their next steps and what support they will need to implement them.

2. When they are ready, ask them to share their ideas with a partner, taking five minutes each. The partner's task is to listen and to ensure the steps chosen are realistic and, where they are not, to help them to make them so.

3. Hand out the action planning sheet and ask people to fill it in.

4. If you are working with a whole governing body ask them to draw up a joint action plan. Alternatively, if people are from different governing bodies start a general discussion on what action people intend to take when they return to their schools.

5. Once action plans are complete, ask people to share their two most important actions in plenary.

Action Planning Sheet

What have I learned on this course?

What do I plan to do regarding the development of my school SRE policy:
- with my governing body?

- with my school?

What are the opportunities?

What support can I get to address any challenges?

What do I want to achieve?

How will I know I have achieved what I wanted to achieve?

Appendix 1

Sex and relationships education: Support for school governors

School governors have a statutory responsibility for sex and relationships education (SRE) in their school. This factsheet explains what SRE is and provides answers to the questions frequently asked by school governors.

What is SRE?

SRE aims to inform children and young people about relationships, emotions, sex, sexuality and sexual health. It enables them to develop personal and social skills and a positive attitude to sexual health and well-being.

SRE starts at home and is received from friends, television, films, magazines and school. It doesn't just happen when we're young: all through our lives we continue to learn about sex and relationships.

SRE in schools is best planned as part of Personal, Social and Health Education (PSHE) and Citizenship and Healthy School development. The context for PSHE and Citizenship is set by the aims of the revised National Curriculum (DfEE/QCA 1999) which requires schools to provide opportunities for all pupils to learn and achieve; promote pupils' spiritual, moral, social and cultural development; and prepare all pupils for the opportunities and responsibilities of life.

It isn't just about sex, it's about relationships, and how people deal with each other.
primary school teacher

SRE Guidance and legislation

The 1996 Education Act consolidated all relevant previous legislation. In summary:

- The SRE elements in the National Curriculum Science Order across all key stages are mandatory for all pupils of primary and secondary school age.
- All schools must have an up to date policy that describes the content and organisation of SRE provided outside the National Curriculum Science Order. It is the school governors' responsibility to ensure that the policy is developed and made available to parents for inspection.
  - Primary schools should either have a policy statement that describes the SRE provided or give a statement of the decision not to provide SRE other than that provided within the National Curriculum Science Order.
  - Secondary schools are required to provide SRE which includes (as a minimum) information about sexually transmitted infections (STIs) and HIV/AIDS.

The SRE Guidance (DfEE 2000) is supported in legislation by the Learning and Skills Act (2000) which requires that:

- young people learn about the nature of marriage and its importance for family life and the bringing up of children;
- young people are protected from teaching and materials which are inappropriate, having regard to the age and the religious and cultural background of the pupils concerned;
- governing bodies have regard to the SRE Guidance.

The SRE Guidance (DfEE, 0116/2000) builds on these legal requirements and states that all schools must have an up to date SRE policy which:

- defines SRE;
- describes how SRE is provided and who is responsible for providing it;
- says how SRE is monitored and evaluated;
- includes information about parents' right to withdrawal;
- is reviewed regularly;
- is available for inspection and to parents.

It also recommends that SRE is planned and delivered as part of PSHE and Citizenship. Schools are expected to have an overall policy on PSHE and Citizenship, which includes SRE. Governing bodies are expected to involve parents, children and young people, and health and other professionals to ensure that SRE addresses the needs of the community, education and health priorities, and the needs of children and young people.

Does SRE have to be taught at our school?

Yes. All schools, including primary schools, are required to have an SRE policy (Education Act 1996) and are recommended to provide it as part of PSHE and Citizenship (SRE Guidance DfEE 0116/2000).

Do special schools have to provide SRE?

Yes. Special and mainstream schools have a duty to ensure that pupils with special educational needs are receiving SRE. The SRE Guidance states SRE should help all pupils understand their physical and emotional development and enable them to make positive decisions in their lives. The Special Educational Needs Code of Practice (DfEE 2001) describes the governing body's responsibilities to 'ensure necessary provision is made for pupils who have special educational needs'. Children and young people with special needs are particularly vulnerable to abuse and SRE can help them to protect themselves now, as well as prepare them for adult life.

Does Ofsted look at SRE?

Ofsted is statutorily required under Section 10 of the School Inspections Act 1996 to evaluate and report on the spiritual, moral, social and cultural development of pupils at any school it inspects. This includes the school's SRE policy. Ofsted (2002) reports that good policies for SRE:

- state the aims and objectives and how the aims will be fulfilled;
- are based on consultation with parents and the wider community;
- establish the framework of values for SRE;
- define the content of SRE and how the needs of individuals will be met, and link to child protection;
- procedures;
- give guidance on teaching methods;
- spell out arrangements for pupils who are withdrawn from aspects of SRE;
- specify the means of review and evaluation and the timetable for these processes.

The Ofsted report provides useful learning outcomes for SRE for all key stages. It challenges schools to be more thorough in their monitoring and evaluation. It recommends that a specialist team delivers SRE and that schools should actively seek pupils' views on SRE. It emphasises the importance of linking SRE with confidential health advice services in school and the wider community. It stresses the importance of planning and delivering SRE that meets the needs of all children and young people, especially those from black and minority ethnic communities, those with a disability, boys, school aged parents and gay young people.

How do we do SRE in a school with religious character?

All schools should ensure that SRE reflects their ethos. They also want children and young people to grow up feeling confident about their emotional and sexual health and with the ability to live alongside people who have different values and beliefs about sex and relationships. Consultation and partnership in planning SRE with pupils, parents and the wider community is key to success. Working together has proved constructive and reassuring to parents and teachers. Talking about the school's values and giving concrete examples of how questions are answered is helpful (Blake and Katrak 2002).

How can SRE fit with all the different cultures represented in our school?

Again it is down to involving and consulting with the whole school community. Difficulties can be caused when assumptions are made. Talking and listening reduces misunderstanding. Many schools start with a fairly limited provision and SRE is further developed as confidence and trust is increased.

Is SRE part of Healthy Schools?

Yes. Each local authority in partnership with its Primary Care Trust (PCT) has developed a local Healthy School Programme, which supports schools with information and training on becoming a healthy school. SRE is one of a number of themes identified by the National Healthy School Standard (NHSS). The NHSS provides criteria and standards to ensure quality and expects schools to develop SRE through a whole school approach, as part of PSHE and Citizenship and in partnership with parents, pupils and community nurses.

How do I get involved with SRE?

Having interest and enthusiasm is a good starting point. A link governor is often selected to work with the school's PSHE and Citizenship Coordinator on policy and curriculum development for SRE. Many governors find the work enjoyable and rewarding. Contact your local Healthy School Programme Coordinator for details of local and national training opportunities and information on the training and video package from the Sex Education Forum (www.ncb.org.uk/sef) and National Association of Governors and Managers (www.nagm.org.uk) – *Developing sex and relationships education in schools: Guidance and training activities for school governors.*

How can we consult with parents?

If you have worked in a genuine partnership with parents, you've consulted them about the policy, made resources open to them, then they are very reassured and actually relieved.
governor advisor

Working in partnership has proven to be very effective in parent/teacher groups, parent/governor groups, parents' evenings or community-based meetings. Clear aims and a planned structure for sessions with parents makes the meeting feel safe. Although most parents want to talk to their children about sex and relationships, they often find it difficult and embarrassing and want schools to help them by providing good SRE. Surveys show 94 per cent of parents/carers support school based SRE (NFER and HEA 1994). Only 0.04 per cent choose to withdraw their children from SRE (Ofsted 2002).

Can parents withdraw their children from SRE?

Parents do not have the right to withdraw their child from the SRE element of the National Science Curriculum. Reproduction is often taught within science. Further information on sex and relationships, skills development and values clarification are provided within PSHE and Citizenship. Parents do have the right to withdraw their child from SRE provided within PSHE and Citizenship.

Your school needs to inform parents and carers about the procedures for requesting that their child is withdrawn, and these should be described in your policy. Involving the whole school community in the development of the SRE policy and programme ensures that withdrawal is rare.

What do we say to parents who want to withdraw their child?

The PSHE and Citizenship Coordinator and/or a senior manager should invite the parent to talk through any concerns and look at the materials used in and aims of SRE. This usually reassures, but if a parent does want to withdraw their child from SRE alternative arrangements will need to be made for the pupil. It may also be appropriate to offer further support to parents. *Developing sex and relationships education in schools: Guidance and training activities for school governors*, an information and training pack from the Sex Education Forum and National Association of Governors and Managers provides a leaflet for parents. Staff may look for support from the governing body in these potentially difficult situations.

If we consult with pupils what are they likely to tell us?

Children and young people tell us that their sex education is too little, too late and too biological and that the adults in their lives are too embarrassed or lack skills and knowledge. Children and young people want SRE where they can talk about feelings and relationships, have their questions answered in a straightforward way and explore 'real life' dilemmas. Recent government legislation (Education Act 2002) requires schools to listen to children and young people and involve them in the process of running the school.

How can we make sure that pupils get confidential advice and support?

The classroom is a public place, where it is inappropriate to talk about private concerns, but SRE may raise issues where children need extra help and support. Many schools are working with PCTs, Connexions and voluntary advice agencies to establish a health advice service or 'one stop shop' either in school or nearby in the community. These services are popular with pupils and their families as well as teachers, especially in rural areas where access to health services can be limited. Children and young people feel safe about taking a range of anxieties and worries to trained staff (Thistle, S 2003). Confidentiality is assured, and referrals can be made effectively. Child protection issues are also addressed within the locally agreed Child Protection Procedures.

SRE Guidance (DfEE 2000) recommends that schools provide pupils with 'precise details of local confidential advice services'. Schools can provide information through:

- notices on bulletin boards;
- posters on class room walls;
- leaflets;
- information in student welfare;
- booklets;
- PSHE and Citizenship lessons;
- visits from health professionals.

Your local Teenage Pregnancy Coordinator can provide a list of local services.

Can we get help from outside agencies?

People who can help to assess need, talk with parents, develop and plan policy and provision, and provide training and ongoing support include:

- local Healthy School Programme Coordinators;
- local education authority PSHE and Citizenship advisors;
- Teenage Pregnancy Coordinators;
- local and national voluntary agencies;
- local health professionals including community nurses.

Is it true that teenage pregnancy rates are high and sexual health is poor?

> *'To have the highest teenage pregnancy rate in Europe is not acceptable. To do nothing is not acceptable.'*
> secondary school head teacher

Teenage pregnancy rates are high, but they are decreasing now that we have a strong 10-year Teenage Pregnancy Strategy (SEU 1999). Ninety thousand girls and young women under 19 get pregnant every year, 7,000 of whom are under 16. The rates of sexually transmitted infections (STIs) among young people, including HIV, continues to rise.

International and national research shows that SRE improves sexual health and well-being, reduces the teenage pregnancy rate, encourages young people to start having sex later, and reduces embarrassment, prejudice and discrimination – if it is provided by trained teachers and other adults who are informed, confident in using a range of learning activities and have an open and positive attitude to sexual health and well-being. SRE also needs to be linked to and coordinated with local sexual health services (HDA 2003).

Where do we start?

The following process is helpful in reviewing SRE policy:

- Include SRE as an agenda item in a Governors' meeting – ask the PSHE and Citizenship Coordinator to work with you to agree the review process.
- Agree a budget for SRE development and continued professional development of teachers.
- Set up a small SRE working group led by the PSHE and Citizenship Coordinator which includes the link Governor, a pupil, a teacher, a parent, a support staff member and a community nurse or health professional.
- Undertake an SRE audit. The local Healthy Schools Coordinator will support an audit, which identifies what SRE is currently delivered, what works well and what needs developing. This is done in consultation with the wider school community. Many schools are enjoying the results of effective pupil participation or active citizenship in this process. Pupils can develop questionnaires, conduct interviews with other pupils, parents and health professionals either in class groups, through school or class councils and peer education and support activities.
- The PSHE and Citizenship Coordinator, working with the SRE working group, collates audit information, revises and drafts SRE policy and submits it to the governing body for agreement on:
  - planning its dissemination;
  - the method of evaluation;
  - date of next review (SRE policy should be reviewed once every two to three years);
  - budget for resources, training and SRE development.

Model PSHE and Citizenship Policy Framework which integrates SRE

Introduction

Name of school

Date policy was completed

People responsible

Healthy School status

Information about

The school

The consultation process

The aims of PSHE and Citizenship

Why it should be taught

The topics and themes of PSHE and Citizenship include healthy eating and exercise, emotional health and well-being, SRE, drug education, safety, citizenship

How PSHE and Citizenship supports the ethos of the school

How the whole school ethos supports PSHE and Citizenship

How PSHE and Citizenship contributes to Healthy School development

Organisation and planning

Name of the PSHE and Citizenship Coordinator

Who teaches PSHE and Citizenship

How PSHE and Citizenship will meet the needs of all pupils, including those who are marginalised and vulnerable

Where PSHE and Citizenship is taught (for example, in the curriculum, special events)

Teaching methods and approaches

Criteria for resource selection

Staff professional development

How pupils' learning will be assessed, recorded and reported

How to link to, and make pupils aware of pastoral systems and health advisory services in school and the wider community

continued...

Specific issues

Legal aspects relating to SRE, drug education, bullying, child
protection and promoting racial equality

Creating a safe environment for learning and teaching,
confidentiality, boundaries

Ensuring pupil participation and active citizenship, including
peer education

Ensuring partnerships across school with parents and wider
community including agreements for using visitors in the
classroom

Monitoring and evaluation

Who will monitor the implementation of the policy

How the work will be evaluated

When will it next be reviewed, once every two to three years is
advised

Appendices

Guidance on particular issues relevant to SRE can be included
in the appendix

Useful contacts

National Healthy School Coordinators

Contact details are available from your LEA or Health
Development Agency (telephone: 020 7661 3072, website:
www.wiredforhealth.gov.uk).

Teenage Pregnancy Coordinators

Contact details are available from your local authority, PCT,
and the Teenage Pregnancy Unit (telephone: 020 7972 5098,
website: www.teenagepregnancyunit.gov.uk).

Sex Education Forum

Telephone: 020 7843 1901, website: www.ncb.org.uk/sef

References

Blake, S and Katrak, Z (2002) *Faith and Values and Sex and Relationships Education.* NCB

DfES (2001) *The Special Educational Needs Code of Practice*

DfEE (2000) *Sex and Relationship Education Guidance (0116/2000)*

DfEE and QCA (1999a) *The National Curriculum Handbook for primary teachers in England*

DfEE and QCA (1999b) *The National Curriculum Handbook for secondary teachers in England*

DfES (2001) *National Healthy School Standard*

Education Act (1996) *Young People's Entitlement to SRE 532-(1)*

Health Development Agency (2003) *Teenage Pregnancy and Parenthood: A review of reviews*

National Foundation for Educational Research and Health Education Authority (1994) *Parents, Schools and Sex Education*

Ofsted (2002) *Sex and Relationships Education in Schools.* HMSO

Social Exclusion Unit (1999) *Teenage Pregnancy Strategy.* HMSO

Thistle, S (2003) *Secondary Schools and Sexual Health Services. Forging the links.* NCB

Appendix 2

Talk to your children about sex and relationships: support for parents

Children learn about sex from a very young age even if we don't talk with them about it. Many of the things they learn are incorrect, confusing and frightening. In a world where sex is used to sell cars and ice creams, and celebrities' private lives become everybody's business, we can't afford *not* to talk to our children about sex and relationships if we're going to help them make sense of it all.

Of course it isn't always easy. Many of us feel embarrassed and worry that we don't know enough. After all, very few of us had good sex education ourselves. Some of us feel that we're not in a position to talk because our own relationships haven't been so good – and we don't want our children accusing us of 'do as I say, not as I do'.

This leaflet is designed for anybody who is a parent or who cares for children and young people. It will help you to talk to them about sex and relationships.

What is sex and relationships education (SRE)?

It is learning about sex, relationships, sexuality and sexual health. Mostly this happens at home, as well as from friends, television, films, magazines and later at school. It doesn't just happen when we're young: all through our lives we learn new facts and continue to develop values and attitudes about sex and relationships.

What do children and young people say?

Young people say that many parents and teachers are not very good at talking about sex and relationships. They leave it too late and often don't talk about it until children have reached puberty, or young people have started feeling sexual desire – or sometimes until they're already having sex. Children and young people don't just want the biological facts. They want to talk about feelings and relationships, and they want us to answer their questions: Why are boys different from girls? How does your body change as you grow up? Where do babies come from? When do you have sex? How do you say no? Why are some people so prejudiced? How do you catch HIV? How do you know if you want to have sex? Why are people gay? How do you know that you're in love? How do you talk to someone about contraception and safer sex?

Why should parents talk about sex and relationships?

- Children and young people want their parents to be the first person to talk to them about sex and relationships.
- If their families are confident talking about sex and relationships, young people will find it easier to resist peer pressure, express their beliefs and opinions, challenge bullying and be able to understand negative messages about sex and relationships.
- Lots of people feel very uncomfortable about sex and think that it's something to laugh about or feel shameful about. We can change this by talking about it positively and being

honest even when it is difficult and embarrassing.
- Young people who have good sex education at home and at school start sex later and are less likely to have an unplanned pregnancy or to get a sexually transmitted infection.

Countries in Europe, that have supported parents, established SRE in schools and provided sexual health services for young people, have seen many benefits. Fewer teenage girls get pregnant, young people start having sex later, and their sexual health is better.

In England our teenage pregnancy rates are high: 90,000 girls and young women under 19 get pregnant every year, 7,000 of whom are under 16. Nearly half these pregnancies end in abortion. Between a quarter and a third of young people under 16 have sex – and the younger they are, the less likely they are to use contraception or have safer sex. The rates of sexually transmitted infections among young people, including HIV, continue to rise.

The Government is taking action through the Teenage Pregnancy Strategy and the Sexual Health and HIV Strategy to improve sexual health and reduce teenage pregnancy. All schools have been sent Guidance by the Department of Education and Skills on how to deliver SRE in schools.

When should we begin talking about sex and relationships?

Start early. Very small children get all sorts of wrong ideas that frighten and confuse them. Talk with them about their feelings, friendships and relationships in the family. Conversations like this help build their confidence in talking about feelings and relationships – and in the years to come will help them to make sensible decisions about sex and relationships. Use proper names for the body parts, and answer questions truthfully and briefly. Children hate lectures – if they want more information they will ask another question. 'Where did you get me'? Can be answered by saying, 'you grew in a special place in mummy's tummy'. A few years later you may be asked by an incredulous 10 year old: 'Why do people have sex'? And the response could be: 'grown ups like to do it because it feels nice, it's a way of showing love and it can make babies'.

Without frightening them make sure that they understand that they can say 'no' to someone who is touching them or approaching them in a way that makes them feel unhappy or uncomfortable. They must also be assured that if something like this happens it is right to tell someone and ask for help.

How do I get started?

- First prepare yourself – talk with your partner, friends and relatives to build up your confidence.
- Read a book or leaflet aimed at your child's age group to increase your knowledge, and help you find words and a style you're comfortable with.

Some Dos and Don'ts

Do

- Read books, leaflets or watch a video with your child.
- Talk while you're doing something else – washing up, driving in the car or fishing.
- Enjoy it. Laugh with each other, not at each other – it can reduce embarrassment and stress.
- Listen rather than judge. Try asking them what they think?
- Answer questions and don't be afraid to say: 'I really don't know – let's work it out or look it up together'. Have a phrase for awkward moments, such as: 'That's a good question, but let's talk about it once we get home' (then make sure you do!).
- Always respond, if you don't, she or he may think it is wrong to talk to you about sex and relationships and as a result you may find your child clams up when you raise the subject.
- If it all feels too personal, try talking about people in books, films and favourite television programmes such as soaps.

Don't

- Bombard your child with questions or talk too much. Many children say it is awful to get the formal lecture on sex or questions fired at them. 'I asked a question and she immediately came back with "Are you having sex then?"' Try and hold on to your anxieties, answer the question, and respect privacy. Young people go through phases of wanting to be private. It's better to keep their trust than antagonise or alienate them.
- Be afraid to tell children what you think, and why. But do try and avoid making harsh judgements of others and give your child some leeway to come to their own opinions.

How to talk with children and young people about values and morality

The family has a major role in developing a child's values and attitudes to sex and relationships. Close loving relationships are the best way of showing a child or young person how your family 'does things', based on your values, culture, faith and beliefs. Research across the world confirms that telling young people to 'say no' to sex doesn't work. Young people don't always want to be told what to do but they are interested in talking about what is right and wrong. Conversations need to be relaxed, realistic and relevant to young people's life experiences.

What do schools do about sex and relationships education?

In the early years up to the age of 7, teachers will be helping children to develop the skills of listening and caring as well as talking about feelings and their relationships with families and friends. Children will learn the names of the body parts, the differences between male and female and the ways in which they will develop and grow. Importantly, they will also learn to recognise unsafe and risky situations, and to ask for help.

> *We address the bodily changes children are going through as they reach the age of 9 and 10 because children are maturing earlier now.*
> primary school head teacher

From 7 to 18 years they will continue to develop their knowledge and skills. In agreement with parents, children will be prepared for the physical and emotional changes of puberty and learn about reproduction and sexual behaviour.

They will also learn about relationships, sexuality, contraception and safer sex, including the importance of family, marriage and stable long-term relationships for the care and support of children. They will also learn social skills, which will help them to be assertive, ask questions, access support, negotiate within relationships, problem solve and make and carry out decisions.

There are laws which ensure that SRE is delivered within a moral framework that values the diversity of family life. The Government has given guidance to each school on how they should teach SRE to ensure that it works by improving sexual heath and well-being, reducing teenage pregnancy and delaying first sex.

All schools are expected to join their local accredited Healthy Schools scheme. This offers a process that ensures SRE is planned in partnership with parents, pupils and school nurses.

How can parents help schools?

Schools review their SRE policy on a regular basis. They are encouraged to work in partnership with parents. Ask the teachers if you can help. Read the policy and look at some of the resources. Parent Teacher Associations or Boards of Governors have meetings on SRE. Try to attend them, and help the school to plan good sex and relationships education. In some areas, parents have been trained as peer sex educators so they can help other parents to talk with children and young people about sex and relationships. Parents can test out leaflets and videos at home, conduct a survey to work out what everybody – both parents and pupils – expect of SRE in school and give classroom talks about being a parent.

What happens if I am not happy with SRE provided in our school?

It is very rare that parents are unhappy with SRE in school. Most concerns are founded on misunderstanding rather than complete disagreement. Where there are concerns, difficulties can often be resolved by making an appointment to talk with the Personal, Social and Health Education (PSHE) and Citizenship Coordinator in school. Be prepared to express your view and hear the views of teachers and governors. And most importantly, listen to what your child thinks. Parents of some cultures and faiths have expressed concerns that boys and girls are taught together. Where this has happened the school has resolved it, by making arrangements to deliver the more private aspects of SRE in single sex groups.

In the rare event that you are still not satisfied, you have the right to withdraw your child from certain lessons or the whole programme provided within PSHE. The reproductive elements of SRE are often delivered in Science and children cannot be withdrawn from a National Curriculum subject. You will need to notify the Chair of Governors and the school will make separate arrangements for your child. Think carefully about how your child will get the right information and education before you withdraw your child completely. It is usually better to hear something from a teacher than hear it in the playground.

What laws about sex affect young people?

Young people cannot legally consent to sex until they are 16. The Department of Health and medical professional guidelines require doctors to offer all patients, including young people under 16, a confidential service. They always encourage young people to talk with their parents, but they are able to give confidential contraceptive advice and treatment if they believe the young person will have sex anyway and endanger their sexual health. Doctors are required to use their professional judgement to assure themselves that the young person is mature enough to understand contraceptive treatment. They are only able to break confidence in very specific circumstances, such as suspected sexual abuse.

Who should be talking about sex and relationships?

Fathers as well as mothers need to talk about sex. Mothers talk more to girls, and often boys feel left out. If we want young men to take responsibility for their sexual behaviour we need to offer them support. One young man commented: 'The moment it looked as if the conversation was going that way Dad was up and out saying he had to mow the lawn,' while another said: 'It was great. They didn't always know the answers but Mum and Dad were always willing to talk with us about it.' Grandparents can play an important role by recalling how it was for them when they were younger. Aunties are often good at talking about these matters with their nephews and nieces. Stepparents and foster parents should also be willing to answer questions and involve themselves in family discussions about sex and relationships, and of course teachers and school nurses will talk to children and young people in school.

My child has a disability. How should I talk about sex and relationships?

Children with learning and/or physical disabilities need exactly the same sex and relationships education as all children, but it may need to be explained more simply and more often. It is also important because they may be more vulnerable to abuse and exploitation. There are some extremely useful resources to get you started (see sources of support, below).

What if my son or daughter is gay?

Even though it may be hard for you it is important that you don't express strong negative feelings because your child will need your acceptance and love and positive messages from you that being gay is fine. Gay children and young people are often bullied verbally and physically, in and out of school. We need to challenge prejudice because it damages the self-esteem and emotional development of the child who is bullied – as well as the bullies themselves. There is information and support available both for you and your child (see sources of support).

I'm a foster parent, and some of the children I look after have been sexually abused. What should I do?

Everything in this leaflet is relevant to you, but the children you're looking after may find that talking about sex brings up traumatic memories. This means you have to build their trust first. They may not know as much about sex as you think – and past abuse may mean they'll be more open to abusive relationships in the future. Reassure them that the abuse was not their fault, be very boundaried and let them know you recognise how painful it is for them. Make sure you get specialist support from the social worker, who may be able to offer training or leaflets for you and the children.

I'm on my own with a son and a daughter; do I need to do anything different?

No, you may feel it's harder because you can't share the responsibility. Try and make sure that your children can talk with trusted family members and friends of both sexes.

I feel I've left it too late to start talking about sex and relationships

It's never too late. Why not start now by talking about this leaflet?

Sources of support

There are many books, leaflets and some videos on sex and relationships, aimed at all ages. They can be borrowed from schools or public libraries, or bought from your local high street book shop. Attend school meetings and events, which will talk about SRE. You'll find that most parents are, like you, trying to do the best for their child. The following organisations offer information, helplines, leaflets, and books and in some cases a mail order service.

Brook
Telephone: 0800 0185023 (for local information)
Website: www.brook.org.uk

FFLAG (Families and Friends of Lesbians and Gays)
Helpline: 01454 852 418
E-mail: info@fflag.org.uk
Website: www.fflag.org.uk

fpa (formally Family Planning Association)
Helpline: 0845 310 1334
Website: www.fpa.org.uk

Parenting Education and Support Forum
Information Service: 020 7284 8388
E-mail: pesf@dial.pipex.com
Website: www.parenting-forum.org.uk

Parentline Plus
Helpline: 0808 800 2222
Website: www.parentlineplus.org.uk

RELATE
Helpline: 0845 456 1310
Fax: 01788 535 007

Appendix 3

Suggested SRE learning outcomes from Ofsted

In their recent report on SRE provision in maintained schools, Ofsted noted that assessment of learning is an area for development in many schools. To support teachers in planning and assessing SRE provision they provided a list of suggested learning objectives organised by key stage.

These learning objectives are incredibly useful in terms of knowledge and understanding as well as values clarification. The Sex Education Forum endorses the following Ofsted learning outcomes and in addition emphasises the importance of emotional and social skills development in SRE and across all aspects of PSHE and Citizenship:

- asking for and offering help
- identifying and naming emotions
- being a good friend
- listening
- giving an opinion
- accessing services
- negotiation
- decision making
- forgiving
- being empathic
- critical thinking
- using condoms and contraception effectively.

By the end of Key Stage 1

Pupils will be able to:

- recognise and compare the main external parts of the bodies of humans*;
- recognise similarities and differences between themselves and others and treat others with sensitivity*;
- identify and share feelings with others;
- recognise safe and unsafe situations;
- identify and be able to talk to someone they trust;
- be aware that their feelings and actions have an impact on others;
- make a friend, talk with him or her and share feelings;
- use simple rules for dealing with strangers and for resisting pressure when they feel uncomfortable or at risk.

Pupils will know and understand:

- that animals, including humans, grow and reproduce*;
- that humans and animals can produce offspring and these grow into adults*;
- the basic rules for keeping themselves safe and healthy;
- about safe places to play and safe people to be with;
- the needs of babies and young people;
- ways in which they are like and different from others;
- that they have some control over their actions and beliefs;
- the names of the main external parts of the body including agreed names for the sexual parts;
- why families are special for caring and sharing.

Pupils will have considered:

- why families are special;
- the similarities and differences between people;
- how their feelings and actions have an impact on other people.

*Part of the National Curriculum for science.

By the end of Key Stage 2

Pupils will be able to:

- express opinions, for example, about relationships and bullying;
- listen to and support others;
- respect other people's viewpoints and beliefs;
- recognise their changing emotions with friends and family and be able to express their feelings positively;
- identify adults they can trust and who they can ask for help;
- be self-confident in a wide range of new situations, such as seeking new friends;
- form opinions that they can articulate to a variety of audiences;
- recognise their own worth and identify positive things about themselves;
- balance the stresses of life in order to promote both their own mental health and well-being and that of others;
- see things from other people's viewpoints, for example their parents and their carers;
- discuss moral issues;
- listen and support their friends and manage friendship problems;
- recognise and challenge stereotypes, for example in relation to gender;
- recognise the pressure of unwanted physical contact, and know ways of resisting it.

Pupils will know and understand:

- that the life processes common to humans and other animals include growth and reproduction*;
- about the main stages of human life*;
- that safe routines can stop the spread of viruses including HIV;

- about the physical changes that take place at puberty, why they happen and how to manage them;
- the many relationships in which they are involved;
- where individual families and groups can find help;
- how the media impact on forming attitudes;
- about keeping themselves safe when involved in risky activities;
- that their actions have consequences and be able to anticipate the results of them;
- about different forms of bullying people and the feelings of both bullies and victims;
- why being different can provoke bullying and know why this is unacceptable;
- about, and accept, a wide range of different family arrangements, for example, second marriages, fostering, extended families and three or more generations living together.

Pupils will have considered:

- the diversity of lifestyles;
- others' points of view, including their parents' or carers';
- why being different can provoke bullying and why this is unacceptable;
- when it is appropriate to take a risk and when to say no and seek help;
- the diversity of values and customs in the school and in the community;
- the need for trust and love in established relationships.

* Part of the National Curriculum for science.

By the end of Key Stage 3

Pupils will be able to:

- manage changing relationships;
- recognise the risk to personal safety in sexual behaviour and be able to make safe decisions;
- ask for help and support;
- explain the relationship between their self-esteem and how they see themselves;
- develop skills of assertiveness in order to resist peer pressure and stereotyping;
- see the complexity of moral, social and cultural issues and be able to form a view of their own;
- develop good interpersonal skills to sustain existing relationships as they grow and change and to help them make new relationships;
- develop empathy with the core values of family life in all its variety of forms;
- recognise the need for commitment, trust and love in meaningful relationships which may manifest themselves in a variety of forms, including marriage;
- recognise the stages of emotions in relation to loss and change caused by divorce, separation and new family members and how to manage their feelings positively.

Pupils will know and understand:

- that fertilisation in humans is the fusion of a male and a female cell*;
- the physical and emotional changes that take place during adolescence*;
- about the human reproductive system, including the menstrual cycle and fertilisation*;
- how the foetus develops in the uterus*;
- how the growth and reproduction of bacteria and replication of viruses can affect health*;

- how the media influence understanding and the attitudes towards sexual health;
- how good relationships can promote mental well-being;
- the law relating to sexual behaviour of young people;
- the sources of advice and support;
- about when and where to get help, such as at a genito-urinary medicine clinic.

Pupils will have considered:

- the benefits of sexual behaviour within a committed relationship;
- how they see themselves affects their self-confidence and behaviour;
- the importance of respecting difference in relation to gender and sexuality;
- how it feels to be different and be discriminated against;
- issues such as the costs of early sexual activity;
- the unacceptability of prejudice and homophobic bullying;
- what rights and responsibilities mean in relationships.

* Part of the National Curriculum for science.

By the end of Key Stage 4

Pupils will be able to:

- recognise the influences and pressures around sexual behaviour and respond appropriately and confidently seek professional health advice;
- manage emotions associated with changing relationships with parents and friends;
- see both sides of an argument and express and justify a personal opinion;
- have the determination to stand up for their beliefs and values;
- make informed choices about the pattern of their lifestyle which promotes well-being;

- have the confidence to assert themselves and challenge offending behaviour;
- develop qualities of empathy and sympathy and the ability to respond emotionally to the range and depth of feelings within close relationships;
- work cooperatively with a range of people who are different from themselves.

Pupils will know and understand:

- the ways in which hormonal control occurs, including the effects of the sex hormones and some medical uses of hormones including the control and promotion of fertility*;
- the defence mechanisms of the body*;
- how sex is determined in humans*;
- how HIV and other STIs affect the body;
- the link between eating disorders and self-image and sexual identity;
- the risks of early sexual activity and the link with the use of alcohol;
- how the different forms of contraception work and where to get advice;
- the role of statutory and voluntary organisations;
- the law in relation to sexual activity for young people and adults;
- how their own sexual identity is influenced by both their personal values and those of their family and society;
- how to respond appropriately within a range of social relationships;
- how to access the statutory and voluntary agencies which support relationships in crisis;
- the qualities of good parenting and its value to family life;
- the benefits of marriage or a stable partnership in bringing up children;
- the way different forms of relationships including marriage depend for their success on maturity and commitment.

Pupils will have considered:

- their developing sense of sexual identity and feel confident and comfortable with it;
- how personal, family and social values influence behaviour;
- the arguments around moral issues such as abortion, contraception and the age of consent;
- the individual contributions made by partners in a sustained relationship and how these can be of joy or benefit to both;
- the consequences of close relationships including having children and how this will create family ties which impact on their lives and those of others.

*Part of the National Curriculum for science.

Appendix 4

Topic cards for Activity E

Twenty-two topic cards are supplied here. Please choose the cards that are relevant. Spare cards have been provided to allow you to add locally relevant topics.

FRIENDSHIPS	RELATIONSHIPS
LOVE	FEELINGS
RIGHTS	RESPONSIBILITIES

PARENTING	NAMES OF BODY PARTS
PUBERTY	PERIODS
HYGIENE	MASTURBATION

GAY SEXUALITY	SEXUAL INTERCOURSE
SAFER SEX	CONCEPTION
CONTRACEPTION	ABORTION

SEXUALLY TRANSMITTED INFECTIONS

HIV/AIDS

MARRIAGE

FAMILY

Appendix 5

Clarifying the law and guidance affecting SRE: answers to quiz in Activity F

ANSWERS

Where there is no reference the answer is based on the DfES SRE Guidance which governors are required to have regard for by the Learning and Skills Act 2000.

1. **School governors have an overall responsibility for determining policy on both the content and organisation of SRE within the school.**

   TRUE

It is a legal requirement for governors of all county and maintained schools to ensure that the school has a SRE policy.

> to make, and keep up-to-date, a separate written statement of their policy with regard to the content and organisation of the relevant part of the curriculum and to ensure that it is made available to parents for inspection
> Education Act 1996 Section 371-(3)

In addition The Learning and Skills Act (2000) requires governors to have regard for the SRE Guidance (DfEE 0116/2000).

2. **Governors are expected to work in partnership with the head teacher, pupils, staff, parents and health professionals and others from the wider community.**

   TRUE

SRE Guidance (0116/2000 DfEE) recommends that SRE is developed as part of PSHE and Citizenship and governors are expected to work in partnership with the whole school community to achieve this. Recent government legislation (Education Act 2002) requires schools, governing bodies and LEAs to listen to children and young people and involve them in the process of running the school. Guidance is forthcoming.

3. **Homosexuality is included throughout SRE.**

   TRUE

Regarding homosexuality, the SRE Guidance (0116/2000) states that:

> young people whatever their developing sexuality need to feel that sex and relationship education is relevant to them and sensitive to their needs . . . [and] that teachers should be able to deal honestly and sensitively with sexual orientation, answer appropriate questions and offer support

Schools are also expected to deal with homophobic bullying. Section 28 was never relevant to schools and has now been repealed.

4. **Contraception and abortion are included in SRE.**

   TRUE

Trained staff in secondary schools are able to give young people full information about different types of contraception, including emergency contraception and their effectiveness.

DfES Guidance states when talking about abortion that:

> the challenge is to offer young people the
> opportunity to explore the dilemmas, enable them to
> know and understand about abortion, and develop
> the communication skills to discuss it with parents
> and health professionals

It also states that 'Young people need access to and precise information about confidential contraceptive information, advice and services'.

5. SRE should link with the sexual health services in the school and in the wider community.

TRUE

Schools are expected to work in partnership with health colleagues. SRE Guidance also encourages secondary schools to provide full information about confidential contraception: 'Young people need access to and precise information about confidential contraceptive information, advice and services'. Also the needs of pupils who are lesbian, gay or bisexual need to be considered:

> young people whatever their developing sexuality
> need to feel that sex and relationship education is
> relevant to them and sensitive to their needs ...
> [and] that teachers should be able to deal honestly
> and sensitively with sexual orientation, answer
> appropriate questions and offer support.

All children and young people are also entitled to general health advice and support and schools are expected to give information on services in the community and helplines such as ChildLine.

6. **Schools catering for students with special educational needs are expected to provide SRE.**

   TRUE

Mainstream schools and special schools have a duty to ensure that children with special educational needs and learning difficulties are properly included in sex and relationship education. SRE Guidance states that SRE 'should help all pupils understand their physical and emotional development and enable them to make positive decisions in their lives'.

7. **Parents have the statutory right to withdraw their children from SRE.**

   TRUE

Parents have the right to withdraw their children from the non-statutory elements of SRE but not from the elements delivered as part of the National Curriculum. For instance, reproduction is taught in Science, and debates on ethical issues related to SRE may be delivered in Citizenship, which became statutory in secondary schools in 2001. Governors are required to ensure that the SRE policy sets out the procedures for withdrawal and ensure alternative arrangements are made for pupils in such cases. The DfES offers schools information for parents who withdraw their children from sex and relationship education (Education Act 1996).

8. **All children have a statutory entitlement to SRE.**

   FALSE

SRE Guidance sets out an expectation for all schools to provide SRE within the context of PSHE and Citizenship. The National Teenage Pregnancy Strategy emphasises SRE as a major component of its 10-year action plan. But the Framework for PSHE and Citizenship still lacks a statutory status although it is included in the revised National

Curriculum 2000. The Education Act 1996, Section 353-(1)c requires(i) 'all maintained secondary schools to make provision for sex education' and (ii) primary schools 'to make, and keep up-to-date, a separate written statement.'

There is therefore some apparent ambiguity. However the SRE Guidance which is supported in legislation by the Learning and Skills Act 2000 sets out a very clear framework for all aspects of SRE. It also requires that:

- young people learn about the nature of marriage and its importance for family life and bringing up children;
- young people are protected from teaching materials, which are inappropriate, having regard to the age and the religious and cultural background of the pupils concerned.

9. HIV/AIDS and other sexually transmitted infections are included in SRE.

  TRUE

Section 352-(3) (Education Act 1996) provides that sex education in secondary schools should include education about HIV and AIDS and any other sexually transmitted infection (Education Act 1996).

10. Schools can develop a confidentiality policy.

  TRUE

A confidentiality policy explains the boundaries of teachers' legal and professional roles and responsibilities, which is reassuring for them, children, young people and their parents. SRE Guidance advises schools to have a confidentiality policy. As a general rule teachers can and should keep confidence within an ethos that maintains the child's best interest as paramount. Teachers also have a child protection responsibility and need to work within the school child protection policy if they believe the child is at risk of serious harm. Visitors to the school must work within school policies such as SRE and Child Protection. School nurses and health professionals work within their own ethical guidelines when working individually with pupils in schools. They are expected to work within the SRE policy when delivering SRE in the classroom.

Appendix 6

Useful organisations

Sex Education Forum

The Sex Education Forum is a unique body of over 50 national organisations that promotes children and young people's entitlement to quality SRE. It provides a range of publications available from www.ncb.org.uk/sef. An information service and contact details for training of school governors is available.

Contact
Telephone on 020 7843 1901
E-mail sexeducationforum@ncb.org.uk

The National Association of Governors and Managers (NAGM)

NAGM is a non-political independent organisation of and for school governors, which is consulted by and offers advice to the Government and other national bodies, whilst seeking to work in partnership with other educational interests, and raising issues of concern, both nationally and locally.

Its membership is made up of individuals or groups (usually governing bodies) who serve as school governors or who have an interest in school governance. It provides information, advice and support to members through a five yearly issue of *Governor News*; publication of a wide range of authoritative papers on aspects of governors' responsibilities (from being a new governor to pupil behaviour and discipline); packs of Smart Cards providing succinct summaries of how to manage important aspects of governance; access to its website; and support of the national governor helpline, Governorline (Tel: 08000 722181)

Contact
2nd Floor SBQ1
29 Smallbrook Queensway
Birmingham
B5 4HG

Tel: 0121 643 5787
Fax: 0121 633 7141
E-mail: governorhq@nagm.org.uk
Website: www.nagm.org.uk

National Healthy School Standard

Local Healthy School Coordinators are located in each local authority or PCT. Contact details are available from your local education authority or the Health Development Agency.

Contact
Telephone: 020 7661 3072
Website: www.wiredforhealth.gov.uk

The National PSE Association for Advisers, Inspectors and Consultants (NSCoPSE)

NSCoPSE is the professional organisation for LEA advisers, inspectors and advisory teachers with responsibility for all aspects of personal and social education, including health education and citizenship. Its membership also includes independent consultants and inspectors, as well as health promotion professionals.

NSCoPSE provides a national forum for the views and interests of those with the responsibility for supporting, monitoring and evaluating personal and social education in schools and colleges throughout England and Wales.

Contact
E-mail: info@nscopse.org.uk
Website: www.nscopse.org.uk

National Health Education Group (NHEG)

NHEG believes that effective Personal, Social and Health Education (PSHE) and Citizenship equips young people with the knowledge, skills and understanding to make informed choices about their lives. It enables young people to build their self-esteem and thus contributes to their academic and social achievements.

The NHEG is an organisation for teaching of professionals involved in the PSHE and Citizenship of children and young people in formal and informal settings. Its purposes are to:

- promote PSHE and Citizenship
- inform, influence and implement national and local policy
- provide personal and professional development opportunities and support for members.

NHEG believes that training for adults should be undertaken continually to build confidence and competence to meet new challenges and opportunities.

Contact
Jan Goulstone
Chair
School Improvement Service
Cambridge House
Cambridge Grove
LONDON
W6 0LE

Telephone: 020 8753 3611
Fax: 020 8753 2879

The KOSH

The Kosh is a performing arts production company, which specialises in creating live theatre performances and community education video programmes.

Contact
Telephone: 020 7263 741
Website: www.ithekosh@dircon.co.uk

Teenage Pregnancy Coordinators

Teenage Pregnancy Coordinators are located within each local authority. Contact details are available from the local authority, PCT, and the Teenage Pregnancy Unit.

Contact
Telephone: 020 7972 5098
E-mail: teenagepregnancyunit@dfes.gsi.gov.uk
Website: www.teenagepregnancyunit.gov.uk

TeacherNet

TeacherNet is a dedicated learning and development resource for teachers of PSHE and Citizenship. It is designed for experienced and new PSHE teachers alike. It contains a flexible, interactive tool to help identify a teacher's development needs; a signpost to 'learning pathways'; a database of resources; and the opportunity to share ideas, seek advice and contribute good practice through the bulletin board.

Contact
Website: www.teachernet.gov.uk/pshe

Appendix 7

Useful resources

Key government documents and resources

Department for Education and Employment (2000) *Sex and Relationship Education Guidance* (0116/2000)

Department for Education and Employment and Qualifications and Curriculum Authority (1999) *The National Curriculum Handbook for primary school teachers in England*

Department for Education and Employment and Qualifications and Curriculum Authority (1999) *The National Curriculum Handbook for secondary school teachers in England*

Department of Health and Department for Education and Employment (1999) *National Healthy School Standard: Guidance*

Department of Health and Department for Education and Employment (1999) *National Healthy School Standard: Getting Started*

Department of Health and Department of Education and Employment (2000). *National Healthy School Standard: Sex and relationships education (SRE).*

Ofsted (2002) *Sex and relationships*

Qualifications and Curriculum Authority (2000) *Personal, Social and Health Education and Citizenship at Key Stages One and Two. Initial guidance for schools*

Qualifications and Curriculum Authority (2000) *Personal, Social and Health Education at Key Stages Three/Four. Initial guidance for schools*

Qualifications and Curriculum Authority (2001) *Personal, Social and Health Education and Citizenship: Teaching and assessing the curriculum for pupils with learning difficulties*

Qualifications and Curriculum Authority (2000) *Citizenship Education at Key Stages Three/Four. Initial guidance for schools*

Sex Education Forum resources

All of the following resources are available from the National Children's Bureau 020 7843 6000 or via the NCB online bookshop at www.ncb-books.org.uk

Scott, L (1996) *Partnership with parents in sex education: A guide for schools and those working with them.* Sex Education Forum

Lenderyou, G, and Ray, C (eds) (1997) *Let's hear it for the boys! Supporting Sex and Relationships Education for boys and young men.* Sex Education Forum

Patel-Kanwal, H and Frances-Lenderyou, G (1998) *Let's talk about sex and relationships: A policy and practice framework for working with children and young people in public care.* Sex Education Forum

Royal National Institute for the Blind and Health Education Authority and Sex Education Forum (2000) *Sexual Health Resources for working with children and young people who are visually impaired and blind*

Blake, S (2001) *Sex and relationships education curriculum resources for Key Stages 3 and 4 PSHE and Citizenship.* Award Scheme Development Accreditation Network/Sex Education Forum/National Children's Bureau

Blake, S and Frances, G (2001) *Just Say No! To abstinence education: Lessons learnt from a sex education study tour to the United States.* Sex Education Forum and National Children's Bureau

Blake, S (2002) *Sex and Relationships Education – a step by step guide for teachers.* David Fulton Publishers

Blake, S and Katrak, Z (2002) *Faith, Values and Sex and Relationships Education.* Sex Education Forum

Sex Education Forum (2002) *Sex, myths and education: Young people talking about sex and relationships education. A video resource.* Sex Education Forum and National Children's Bureau and The Kosh

Sense, Sex and Relationships, an imaginative and interactive CD Rom that covers all aspects of sex and relationships. It has a section that focuses specifically on SRE in schools.(2003)

Thistle, S (2003) *Secondary schools and sexual health services: Forging the links.* Sex Education Forum.

Blake, S and Katrak, Z (2003 forthcoming) *Ethnicity, culture and sex and relationships education.* Sex Education Forum

The Sex Education Forum produces a range of factsheets, which are designed to offer accessible and practical digests of current research and ideas. Each factsheet focuses on a specific aspect of SRE. For a full list of titles contact the Sex Education Forum on 020 7843 1901 or visit the website www.ncb.org.uk/sef and download them for free.

Current factsheets available from SEF and NCB include:

- Meeting the needs of boys and young men in sex and relationships education (1997)
- Effective Learning: Approaches to teaching PSHE and citizenship (2003)
- The Framework for Sex and relationships education (1999)

- Meeting the needs of girls and young women in sex and relationships education (2000)
- Taking the initiative: Positive guidance on sex and relationships education in the secondary school (2000)
- Ensuring entitlement: Sex and relationships education for disabled children (2001)
- PSHE and Citizenship – ensuring effective sex and relationships education (2001)
- Sex and Relationships Education in the Primary School (2002)
- A whole school approach to PSHE and Citizenship (2003)

Appendix 8

References

Blake, S and Katrak, Z (2002) *Faith and Values and Sex and Relationships Education.* Sex Education Forum

DfEE (2001) *The Special Educational Needs Code of Practice*

DfEE (2000) *Sex and Relationship Education Guidance* (0116/2000)

DfEE and QCA (1999a) *The National Curriculum Handbook for primary teachers in England*

DfEE and QCA (1999b) *The National Curriculum Handbook for secondary teachers in England*

DfES (2001) *National Healthy School Standard*

Education Act (1996) *Young People's Entitlement to SRE 532-(1)*

Health Development Agency (2003) *Teenage pregnancy and parenthood: A review of reviews*

National Children's Bureau (1999) *Highlight 158 Young people's sexual attitudes and behaviour; a review of research.*

National Foundation for Educational Research (1994). *Parents, schools and sex education: A compelling case for partnership*

Ofsted (2002) *Sex and Relationships*

Social Exclusion Unit (1999) *Teenage Pregnancy Report*

Thistle, S (2003) *Secondary Schools and Sexual Health Services: Forging the links.* Sex Education Forum

Wellings, K (1994). *Sexual behaviour in Britain: the national survey of sexual attitudes and lifestyles*

Appendix 9

Sex Education Forum Member Organisations

APAUSE	www.ex.ac.uk/sshs/apause
Association for Health Education Coordinators (ASHEC)	
AVERT	www.avert.org.uk
Barnardo's	www.barnardos.org.uk
Black Health Agency	www.blackhealthagency.org.uk
British Humanist Association	www.humanism.org.uk
Brook Advisory Centres	www.brook.org.uk
Catholic Education Service	www.catholiceducation.org.uk
Centre for HIV and Sexual Health	www.sexualhealthsheffield.co.uk
ChildLine UK	www.childline.org.uk
Children's Society, The	www.the-childrens-society.org.uk
Church of England Board of Education	www.natsoc.org.uk
Community Practitioners and Health Visitors Association (CPHVA)	www.msfcphva.org
Education for Choice	www.efc.org.uk
Families and Friends of Lesbian and Gays (FFLAG)	www.fflag.org.uk
Foundation for Women's Health, Research and Development (FORWARD)	www.forward@dircon.co.uk
fpa (formally the Family Planning Association)	www.fpa.org.uk
Girlguiding UK	www.guides.org.uk
Image in Action	
Jewish Marriage Council	www.jmc-uk.org

League of Jewish Women	www.leagueofjewishwomen.org.uk
Lesbian and Gay Christian Movement	www.lgcm.org.uk
Marriage Care	www.marriage.org.uk
Medical Foundation for AIDS and Sexual Health	www.medfash.org.uk
MENCAP	www.mencap.org.uk
Methodist Church	www.methodist.org.uk
Mothers Union	www.mothersunion.org.uk
National AIDS Trust (NAT)	www.nat.org.uk
National Association for Governors and Managers (NAGM)	www.nagm.org.uk
National Association for Pastoral Care in Education (NAPCE)	www.warwick.ac.uk/wie/napce
National Children's Bureau	www.ncb.org.uk
National Council of Women of Great Britain	www.ncwgb.org.uk
National Health Education Group (NHEG)	www.nheg.org.uk
National Society for the Prevention of Cruelty to Children (NSPCC)	www.nspcc.org.uk
National Youth Agency	www.nya.org.uk
NAZ Project London	www.naz.org.uk
NCH	www.nch.org.uk
NSCOPSE	www.nscopse.org.uk
OASIS	www.oasistrust.org.uk
One Plus One	www.oneplusone.org.uk
Parenting Education and Support Forum	www.parenting-forum.org.uk
RELATE	www.relate.org.uk
Royal College of Nursing (RCN)	www.rcn.org.uk
Save the Children Fund	www.savethechildren.org.uk
Society of Health Advisors in STD (SHASTD)	www.shastd.org.uk
Society of Health Promotion Specialists	www.hj-web.co.uk/sheps
TACADE	www.tacade.com
Terrence Higgins Trust (THT)	www.tht.org.uk
Trust for the Study of Adolescence (TSA)	www.tsa.uk.com
Working with Men	www.workingwithmen.org
YWCA	www.ywca-gb.org.uk